Cool
Japan

英語訳つき
# おりがみ Best50
青木真理／訳　主婦の友社／編
Origami for Beginners：50 Easy and Fun Japanese Paperfoldings

主婦の友社

# Introduction

## Origami for the world

Japanese traditional art "origami" is now one of the well known Japanese words all over the world. A piece of paper changes its shape into flowers, animals, vehicles and toys. People are fascinated by the transformations. After folding origami, you can enjoy making stories, playing make-believe games, or decorating your room with your original pieces.

In this book, there are 50 popular origami figures which have been loved throughout the ages in Japan. Also, we added English translation so that overseas people may fold easily with the guidance.

Recently, the number of tourists visiting Japan has been increasing remarkably, and because of Japan hosting the Tokyo Olympic and Paralympic Games, the world keeps watch on Japanese culture more and more.

We hope that through this book, many people will come to know the charm of origami.

The paper crane is a typical piece of Japanese origami. There is an old custom that you can wish for peace, long life, and recovery from illness by folding 1,000 paper cranes. And be worthy of note, four paper cranes folded by the former President Obama were displayed in Hiroshima.

つるは日本のおりがみを代表する作品。平和、長寿、病気の回復を祈願して1000羽のつるをおる風習も。オバマ元大統領がおったつるも広島に飾られました。

# はじめに

## おりがみをおる楽しさを世界に

日本の伝統文化おりがみは、そのまま「origami」と訳されて世界中の多くの人に親しまれています。たった1枚の紙が、花や動物、乗り物やおもちゃなどへとさまざまに形をかえていくおもしろさに、誰もがひきこまれるのでしょう。おった作品を使っておはなしをつくったり、ごっこ遊びをしたり、部屋に飾ったり、おった後もたっぷり楽しめるのもおりがみのすばらしさです。

この本には、時代をこえて愛される人気のおりがみ50作品を集めました。海外の人もおれるように、英訳をつけました。

近年、来日観光客が増加し、また、東京オリンピック・パラリンピックの開催もあって、日本文化はますます注目を集めつつあります。

ひとりでも多くの人におりがみの魅力が届きますように。

# Fold it like this
## おりがみは、こうおろう！

All figures have illustrations and explanations so that everyone can follow easily step by step. Refer to "The rules of basic folds and symbols" on pages 6-9 for basic information. Also, each figure has ★ marks indicating the level of difficulty.

( ★ easy, ★★ normal, ★★★ challenging)
In the illustration, the dotted line shows the line to fold along, and the arrow shows the direction in which to fold. If you find yourself at a loss, refer to the next step's illustration. Maybe you can get a hint from the next step's shape. Even if you fold in a wrong way, it's not a failure. The paper is reusable, so get back to the point where you went wrong and refold.

全作品におり方の図と説明がついています。両方を確かめながらおりましょう。図の見方や記号については6ページからの「基本のおり方と記号のルール」を見てください。また各作品に★の数でむずかしさの目安をつけています。

( ★ かんたん ★★ ふつう ★★★ がんばれ)
おり図では基本的に、おる位置を点線で、おる方向を矢じるしで表してあります。もしおり方がわからなくなったら次の図を見ましょう。次の図の形がヒントになっておれることがあります。まちがえておっても失敗ではありません。紙はくり返し使えるので、まちがえたところまでもどっており直しをしましょう。

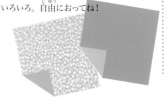

Japanese paper "washi" is a little thick but soft. When you get used to origami, try using this beautiful paper.
少し厚めだけれどやわらかい和紙。おりがみになれたら使ってみよう。

There are various types of paper for origami, such as paper colored on both sides or beautifully patterned paper. Choose the paper you want and enjoy folding any figure you like.
両面おりがみや模様おりがみなど、紙はいろいろ。自由におってね!

# How to make a good fold
## きれいにおるには？

There are two knacks to fold nicely.
**1.** Let the corners or sides meet as closely as possible.
**2.** Make the creases firmly with your fingertips, as though you were pressing with an iron.

きれいにおるコツは2つあります。
**1** 角と角、辺と辺などをなるべく合わせるようにしておる。
**2** おったところを、アイロンをかけるように指先でなぞり、おりすじをしっかりつける。

Try to make the corners and sides meet as closely as possible.
角やふちをなるべく合わせてね。

Press the folded crease firmly.
ギューッとおり目を指でなぞるよ。

# Contents もくじ

## Part 3 ◆ Animals and Plants Origami 生きものおりがみ

## Part 4 ◆ Play 'n' Fun Origami 遊べるおりがみ

# The rules of basic folds and symbols
## 基本のおり方と記号のルール

There are some basic folding rules in origami.
The dotted line shows the line to fold along, and the arrow shows the direction
in which to fold or unfold. There are also some symbols in the illustrations
which show the models to follow.
Remember the rules of basic folds and symbols.

おりがみには、いろいろな基本のおり方があります。点線がおる位置、矢じるしがおる方向を
表しています。また、おるときのお手本となる「おり図」には記号が出てきます。
おり方の基本と記号のルールをおぼえておきましょう。

# Folding inside
## 谷おり

Fold the paper at the dotted line
so that the dotted line is inside.

点線のところが内がわに
「谷」になるようにおります。

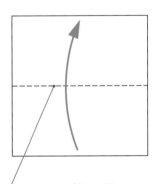

**Folding-in line** 谷おり線

Fold in here in the direction
of the arrow.

この位置で矢じるしのほうへおり、
谷おりをする。

# Folding outside
## 山おり

Fold the paper outward at the
dotted line so that the dotted
line is outside.

点線のところが外がわに
「山」になるようにおります。

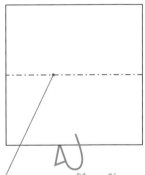

**Folding-out line** 山おり線

Fold outward here in
the direction of the arrow.

この位置で矢じるしのほうへおり、
山おりをする。

6

# Making a crease
## おりすじをつける

**Fold in half to make a crease and unfold. The crease is a guide for the next steps.**

一度<sub>いちど</sub>おってもどすと「おりすじ」が

つきます。おりすじは、次<sub>つぎ</sub>をおるための

ガイドになります。

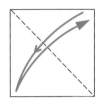

**1** Fold in at the dotted line and unfold.

点線<sub>てんせん</sub>のところでおったら、
開<sub>ひら</sub>いてもどす。

**2** A diagonal crease.

おりすじがついた。

**1** Fold in at the dotted line and unfold.

点線<sub>てんせん</sub>のところでおったら、
開<sub>ひら</sub>いてもどす。

**2** A vertical crease.

おりすじがついた。

---

# When the "making a crease" step is omitted
## 「おりすじをつける」が 省略<sub>しょうりゃく</sub>してあったら

**Fold in as illustrated and unfold.**

図<sub>ず</sub>のとおりにおりすじがつくように、

おってもどしておきます。

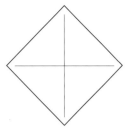

**Fold both top and bottom corners in half and unfold.**

上下<sub>じょうげ</sub>の角<sub>かど</sub>を合<sub>あ</sub>わせて

おってもどす。

**1**

**This time, fold both right and left corners in half and unfold.**

今度<sub>こんど</sub>は左右<sub>さゆう</sub>の角<sub>かど</sub>を
合<sub>あ</sub>わせておってもどす。

**2**

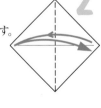

# Opening and flattening
## 開いてつぶす

**Put your finger in the pocket from ⬆.
Open toward the arrow and flatten.**

⬆のあたりからふくろに指を入れます。そ
して矢じるしのほうへ開いたら、つぶします。

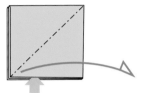

While putting your finger in the
square pocket, it will look like this.

**1** 四角のふくろに指を
入れて開いたところ。

When it is flattened,
it becomes a triangle.

**2** つぶすと三角に。

While putting your finger in the
triangle pocket, it will look like this.

**1** 三角のふくろに指を
入れて開いたところ。

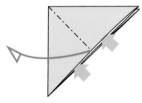

When it is flattened,
it becomes a square.

**2** つぶすと四角に。

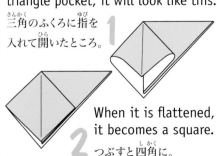

# Inside reverse fold
## 中わりおり

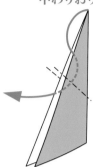

**This is the way to open up the
folded part and fold it inside.**

二つおりの間をわって、おり入れます。

Fold in at the dotted line
to make a crease
and unfold.

上の図のおり線のところで
一度おってもどし、
おりすじをつける。

**1**

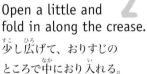

Open a little and
fold in along the crease.

少し広げて、おりすじの
ところで中におり入れる。

**2**

**3** Fold down more
to turn the top
inside out.

もっとおり下げて……

**4** A finished inside
reverse fold.

中わりおりの完成。

# Outside reverse fold
### 外わりおり

This is the opposite of the inside reverse fold.

二つおりを、とちゅうからうら返すようにします。

Fold in at the dotted line to make a crease and unfold.

上の図のおり線のところで一度おってもどし、おりすじをつける。

**1**

Open and fold backward along the crease and reverse.

中を広げて、おりすじのところでペコンとうら返す。

**2**

Fold up tightly to finish the outside reverse fold.

しっかりたたんだら外わりおりの完成。

**3**

# Pleats fold
### だんおり

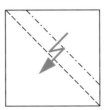

Repeat fold in and out to make some pleats.

おり上がりが「だん」になるように、山おりと谷おりをとなり合わせにおります。

Fold in half at the folding-in line. Fold back at the folding-out line.

まず半分におったら（谷おり）、点線のところでおり返す（山おり）。

**1**

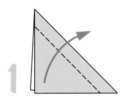

A finished pleats fold.

だんおりの完成。

**2**

# Changing the folding face
### おりずらす

This is the way to change the folding face.

おっている面とちがう面を出します。

Fold in the upper right flap to the left and lower left flap to the right.

手前を左に、向こうがわを右におる。

**1**

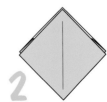

A different face from the one before.

今までおっていたのと別の面が出る。

**2**

9

# Balloon
## ふうせん

**If you blow into it,
it becomes
a square balloon.**

**1** Fold the opposing
two sides in half.
辺と辺を合わせて半分におる。

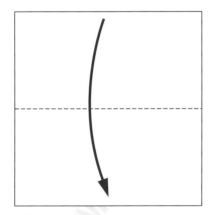

**3** Put your finger in from ⬆.
Pull up the upper flap and
flatten toward the arrow to
make a triangle.

⬆から指を入れ、矢じるしのほうへ
開いて三角につぶす。

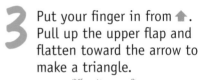

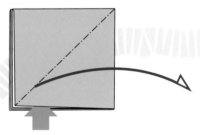

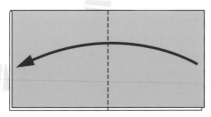

**2** Fold in half again.
もう一度半分におる。

人気おりがみベスト10

Tuck the top corners
into the pockets.
Repeat on the other side.

先をふくろの中におり入れる。

うらも同じに。

**7**

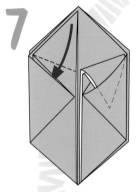

**8**

Blow into it
from the bottom
and make it into
a cubic shape.

下のあなから
息をふき入れ、

ふくらませる。
四角くととのえる。

**Blow**
ふく

**Finished!**
できあがり

Fold in the upper corners to
meet at the center.
Repeat on the other side.

まん中で合うように
両方の角をおる。
うらも同じに。

**6**

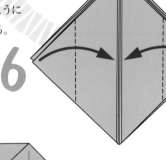

**5**

Fold up the upper corners
to meet at the top.
Repeat on the other side.

両方の角をおり上げる。
うらも同じに。

**4**

After folding **3**, it will look like
this. Repeat on the other side.

**3**をおったところ。
うらも**3**と同じように開いてつぶす。

# House
### いえ

This is a lovely house
with two roofs.
It's fun to draw
a door and some windows.

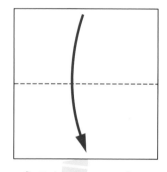

**1** Fold the opposing
two sides in half.
辺と辺を合わせて
半分におる。

After making a crease,
fold in both sides to meet at the center.
図のようにおりすじをつけたら、
左右をおる。

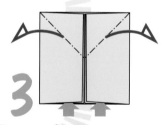

**3** Put your fingers
in the pockets from ⬆.
Pull up and flatten toward
the arrows.
ふくろに⬆から指を入れ、
それぞれ矢じるしのほうへ
開いてつぶす。

## Finished!
できあがり

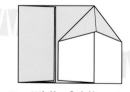

**4** While folding **3**,
it will look like this.

**3**をおっているところ

# ★ Tulip
## チューリップ

人気おりがみベスト10

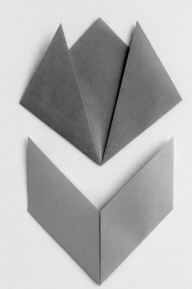

A simple shape, but it's so cute!
Fold the flower
and leaf separately.

## Flower
### 花

**1**

Fold in half
to make a triangle.
角を合わせて半分におる。

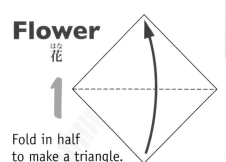

**2** Fold up
both corners.
左右の角を
おり上げる。

## Leaf
### 葉

**1**

Fold in half to
make a triangle.
角を合わせて半分におる。

**2** After making a crease,
fold up the corner.
図のようにおりすじを
つけたら、下の角を
おり上げる。

**3** Fold up both sides
along the crease.
おりすじに合わせて
左右をおり上げる。

## Finished!
### できあがり

13

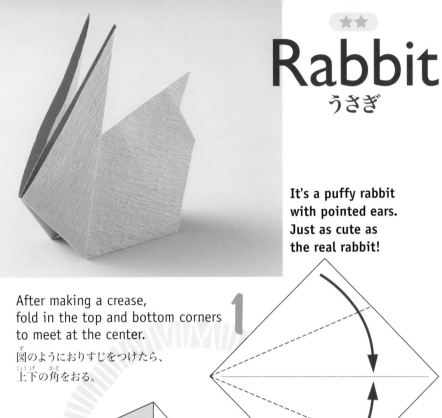

# Rabbit
うさぎ
★★

It's a puffy rabbit
with pointed ears.
Just as cute as
the real rabbit!

**1**

After making a crease,
fold in the top and bottom corners
to meet at the center.

図のようにおりすじをつけたら、
上下の角をおる。

**2**

Fold in the right
corner to meet the joint.

右の角を合わせ目までおる。

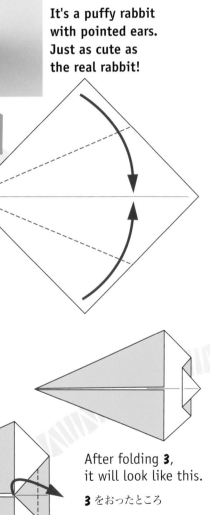

After folding **3**,
it will look like this.

**3** をおったところ

**3**

Fold back
to make the tip stick out.

先がとび出すようにもう一度おる。

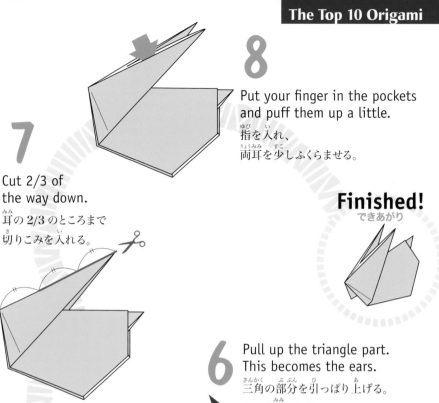

**8**

Put your finger in the pockets
and puff them up a little.
指を入れ、
両耳を少しふくらませる。

**Finished!**
できあがり

**7**

Cut 2/3 of
the way down.
耳の2/3のところまで
切りこみを入れる。

**6**

Pull up the triangle part.
This becomes the ears.
三角の部分を引っぱり上げる。
ここが耳になる。

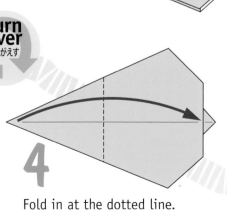

**Turn over**
うらがえす

**4**

Fold in at the dotted line.
うら返したら、点線のところでおる。

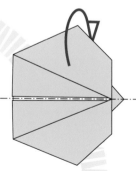

**5**

Fold in half outward
at the dotted line.
向こうがわへ全体を
半分におる。

# ★★ Airplane

## ジェットき

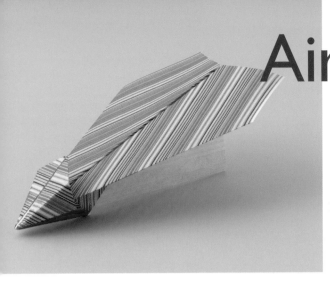

**Look at the top cover!
It's a cool cockpit, isn't it?**

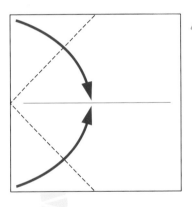

**1** After making a crease,
fold in both left side corners to
meet the crease.
図のようにおりすじをつけたら、
角をおりすじに合わせておる。

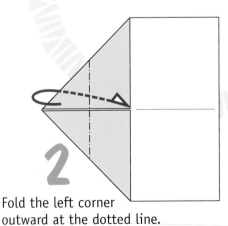

**2** Fold the left corner
outward at the dotted line.
左の角を向こうがわへおる。

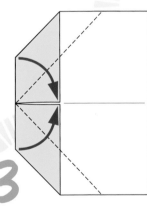

**3** Fold in the left corners
to meet at the center.
おりすじに合わせて
それぞれおる。

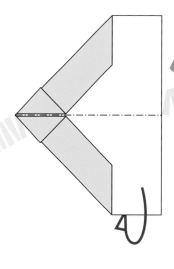

**4** Fold in half outward.
向こうがわへ全体を半分におる。

**5** Fold in at the dotted line.
Repeat on the other side.
点線のところで羽根をおる。
うらも同じに。

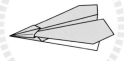

**6** Pull out the corner part
folded between the wings.
中におりこまれている
角を引き出す。

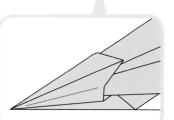

**Finished!**
できあがり

**Let it soar!**
ビュンビュンとばそう!

**How far can it fly?**
どのくらいとぶかな?

17

# Rose

## バラ

**Open the flower petals
one by one.
It's thick and a little bit
hard to fold,
but you can do it!**

## 1

After making
the diagonal creases,
fold in the four corners
to meet at the center.

図のように
おりすじをつけたら、
4つの角を
中心に向けておる。

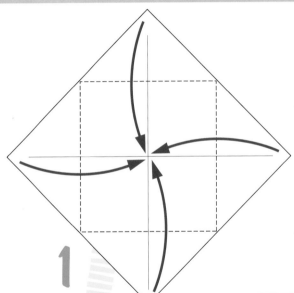

## 2

Fold in
the four corners
again.

4つの角を
もう一度
内がわにおる。

## 3

Fold in the four corners
one more time.

4つの角をさらに内がわにおる。

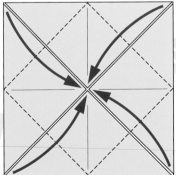

**4** This time,
fold the four corners outward.
今度は角を向こうがわへ山おりにする。

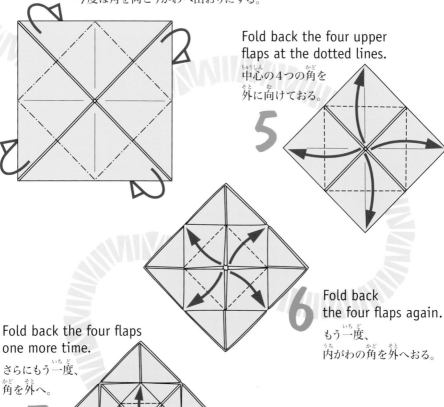

Fold back the four upper
flaps at the dotted lines.
中心の4つの角を
外に向けておる。

**5**

**6** Fold back
the four flaps again.
もう一度、
内がわの角を外へおる。

Fold back the four flaps
one more time.
さらにもう一度、
角を外へ。

**7**

**Finished!**
できあがり

**You can make curls
on the petals with a thin stick.**
細いぼうなどで花びらに
カールをつけると、まるで本物みたいに！

★★★

# Butterfly
## ちょうちょ

This fluttering butterfly
looks like it's dancing
in the flower garden.
Let's draw
some marks on the wings.

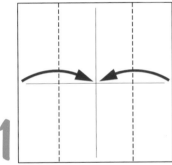

## 1

After making the cross creases,
fold in both opposing sides.

図のようにおりすじをつけたら、
左右をおる。

Fold in both top and bottom sides
to meet the crease.

おりすじに合わせて上下をおる。

## 2

Fold in diagonally
to make two creases.

ななめにおって
おりすじをつける。

## 3

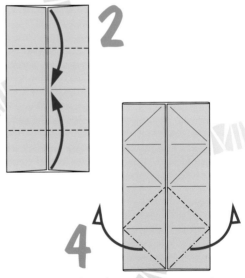

## 4

Unfold to the shape as illustrated,
pull up and flatten toward the arrows.

開いて図の形までもどしたら、
矢じるしのほうへ開いてつぶす。

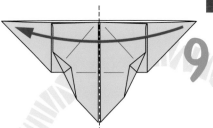

**9** Fold in half.
全体を半分におる。

Fold both sides
at the dotted line
and spread the wings.
表裏とも点線のところでおって、
羽を広げる。

**10**

**8** Fold in both corners of
the upper flap a little.
手前の1枚の角を小さくおる。

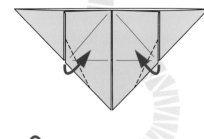

**Finished!**
できあがり

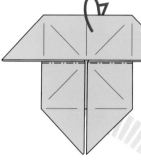

**7**

Fold the top part
outward.
上を向こうがわへおる。

**6** Fold in diagonally
at the dotted lines.
おりすじのところで
ななめにおる。

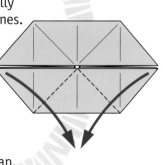

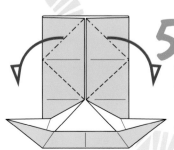

**5**

While folding **4**,
it will look like this.
Repeat on the top flap.
**4** をおっているところ。
上も同じように開いてつぶす。

# Boat
ボート

Turn it inside out and there—you have a 3D boat. It's better to use a soft type of paper like Japanese washi.

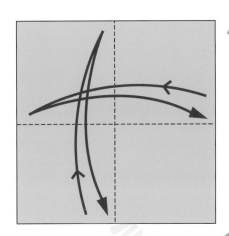

**1** Begin with the colored side up and make the cross creases.
色のついた面を表にして
おりすじをつける。

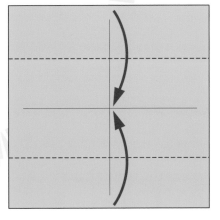

**2** Fold in both top and bottom sides to meet at the center.
おりすじに合わせて上下をおる。

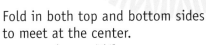

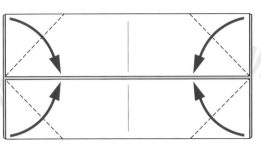

**3** Fold in the four corners at the dotted lines.
4つの角を内におる。

**4** Fold in the four corners at the dotted lines.
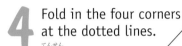
点線のところで
4つの角をおる。

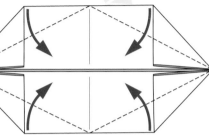

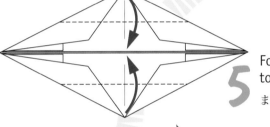

**5** Fold in the top and bottom corners to meet at the center.
まん中で合うように上下の角をおる。

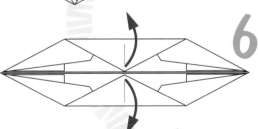

**6** Put your fingers inside and turn it inside out.
おり目の間に指を入れ、
外に開く。

**7** Turn it over carefully so that the colored side is on the outside.
色のついた面が表になるようにさらに開き、
ぐるりとうら返す。

**Finished!**
できあがり

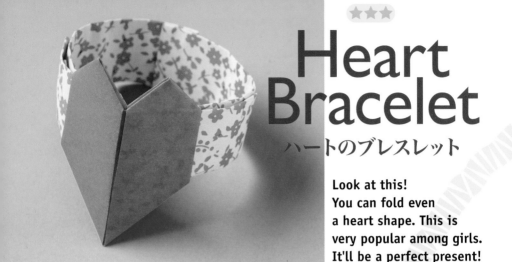

★★★

# Heart Bracelet
## ハートのブレスレット

**Look at this!
You can fold even
a heart shape. This is
very popular among girls.
It'll be a perfect present!**

※ Double-sided paper. 両面おりがみ使用。

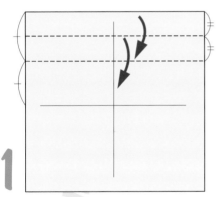

**1**

After making the cross creases,
fold in twice.
図のようにおりすじをつけたら、
まくように2回おる。

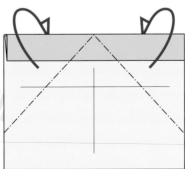

**2**

Fold both corners
outward to meet
at the center.
おりすじに合わせて
向こうがわへおる。

**Turn over**
うらがえす

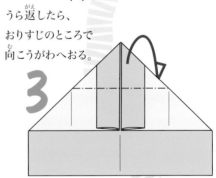

Fold the top part outward.
うら返したら、
おりすじのところで
向こうがわへおる。

**3**

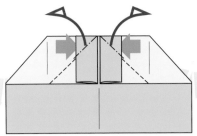

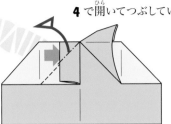

While folding **4**,
it will look like this.

**4**で開いてつぶしているところ

**4** Put your fingers in from ,
pull up and flatten
toward the arrows.

から指を入れ、
矢じるしのほうへ開いてつぶす。

**5**

Fold in both top flaps ○
at the dotted lines
to meet
at the center ◎.

○の辺と◎の
おりすじが合うように、それぞれおる。

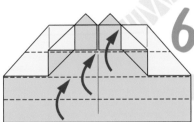

How about wearing
matching
bracelets
with your friend?

お友だちとペアで
持つと楽しいよ。

**6**

Fold up three times
at the dotted lines.

点線のところで
3回まくようにおる。

**Finished!**
できあがり

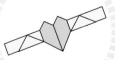

After folding **6**,
it will look like this.

**6**をおったところ

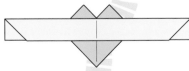

Wind it around
your wrist
and fasten it up.

腕にまいて、輪にとめよう。

**Turn over**
うらがえす

25

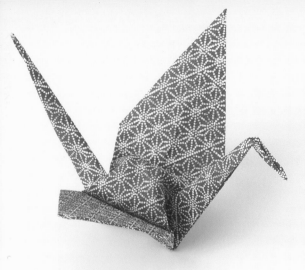

# Crane
## つる

★★★

This beautiful piece is
probably the most famous
Japanese origami.
It is said that your wish
will come true
when you fold 1,000 cranes.

**1** Fold in half
to make a triangle.
角を合わせて
半分におる。

**2** Fold in half again.
角を合わせてもう一度半分におる。

**3** Put your fingers in from ⬆,
open up the flap toward
the arrow and flatten.
⬆から指を入れ、
矢じるしのほうへ開いて四角くつぶす。

**4** Repeat on
the other side.
うらも**3**と
同じように、
開いてつぶす。

While folding **3**,
it will look
like this.
**3**をおっているところ

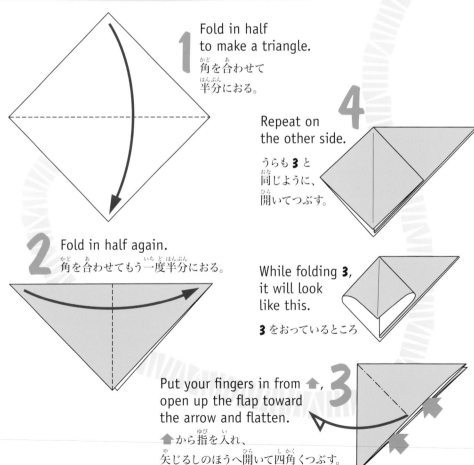

**5**

Make the creases at the dotted lines.

てんせん
点線のところで

おりすじをつける。

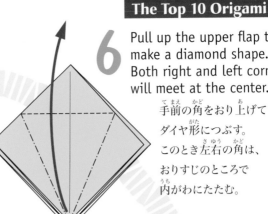

**6**

Pull up the upper flap to make a diamond shape. Both right and left corners will meet at the center.

てまえ　かど　　　あ
手前の角をおり上げて

がた
ダイヤ形につぶす。

　　　　　さゆう　かど
このとき左右の角は、

おりすじのところで

うち
内がわにたたむ。

**7**

While folding **6**, it will look like this. Repeat **5** & **6** on the other side.

**6** をおっているところ。

　　　おな
うらも同じように

**5** 〜 **6** をおる。

**9**

Put your fingers inside the flaps and fold up at the dotted lines. This is the inside reverse fold.

なか
中わりおりで

おお　　　　　　あ
大きくおり上げる。

**8**

Fold in both corners narrowly at the dotted lines. Repeat on the other side.

さゆう　ほそ　　　　　　　おな
左右を細くおる。うらも同じに。

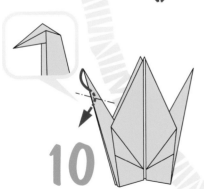

**10**

Use one side of **9** and do the inside reverse fold to make the head.

ちい　　なか　　　　　　あたま
小さい中わりおりで頭をおる。

Spread the wings nicely.

はね
羽をきれいに

ひろ
広げよう。

**Finished!**
できあがり

27

# Humming Top
## ぶんぶんごま

**When you twist the top
and pull the string,
the top will hum as it spins.
This is an ancient Japanese toy.**

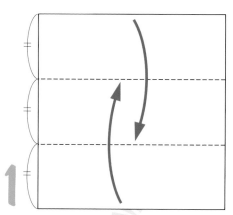

**1**

Ready two pieces of origami.
Fold each paper in three at the dotted lines.

おりがみを2枚用意して、それぞれに **1**〜**2** をおる。
まず三つおりにする。

**2**

Fold in both corners of each paper
at the dotted lines.

点線のところで角をおる。

Put one piece on top of
the other piece as illustrated.
Fold the lower piece top flap
down over the upper piece.

2つを図のように重ねたら、
上の角をおる。

**3**

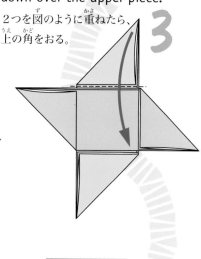

After folding **2**,
it will look like this.

**2** までおったところ

和<sub>わ</sub>の伝統<sub>でんとう</sub>おりがみ

# Let's spin the top!

ぶんぶんごまを回<sub>まわ</sub>して遊<sub>あそ</sub>ぼう！

Hold both ends of the string and twist the top several times. Pull and loosen the string and the top will start spinning and humming.

輪<sub>わ</sub>にしたひもの両<sub>りょう</sub>はしを持<sub>も</sub>って、
何回<sub>なんかい</sub>か回<sub>まわ</sub>してねじろう。
ひもを引<sub>ひ</sub>っぱったりゆるめたりすると、
こまがブンブン回<sub>まわ</sub>るよ！

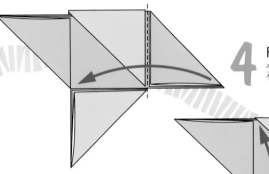

**4** Fold the upper right flap to the left.
右<sub>みぎ</sub>の角<sub>かど</sub>をおる。

**5** Fold the lower bottom flap up over the upper piece.
下<sub>した</sub>の角<sub>かど</sub>をおる。

## Finished!

できあがり

Make two small holes as illustrated, pass a string through them and tie the ends together.
Use fine but strong string (a kite string may do) about 60cm long.

図<sub>ず</sub>のようにあなを2つあけたら、
60cm くらいのじょうぶなひもを通<sub>とお</sub>して輪<sub>わ</sub>にする。

**6** Fold the upper left flap to the right.
左<sub>ひだり</sub>の角<sub>かど</sub>をおる。

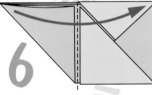

**7** Tuck the tip folded in **6** into the diagonal pocket.
左<sub>ひだり</sub>の角<sub>かど</sub>の先<sub>さき</sub>を中<sub>なか</sub>に入<sub>い</sub>れる。

# Paper Gun
## かみでっぽう

★★

Swing down the paper gun
and it makes a loud pop!
Use large, thin paper,
such as newspaper.

**1**

Ready a rectangular paper, like newspaper.
Fold in half to make a crease and unfold.
新聞紙など長方形の紙を用意する。
横半分におりすじをつける。

**3** Fold in half
at the dotted line.
全体を半分におる。

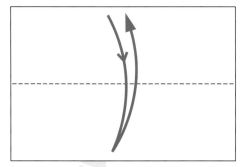

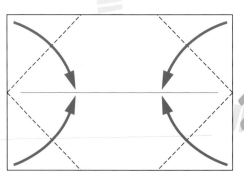

**2** Fold in the four corners
at the dotted lines.
おりすじに合わせて
4つの角をおる。

Put your hand in from ⬆,
pull up the upper flap and
flatten toward the arrow.

ふくろに⬆から手を入れ、
矢じるしのほうへ
開いてつぶす。

**5**

Repeat on
the other side.

もうひとつのふくろも、
同じように
開いてつぶす。

**6**

Fold in half
at the dotted line
again.

全体をさらに半分におる。

**4**

Fold the upper flap
at the dotted line.
Repeat on
the other side.

手前の1枚を
こちらに、うらの
1枚を向こうにおる。

**7**

**Swing it down as hard as
you can and bang!
Tuck in the unfolded part
to do it again.**

元気よくふり下ろして
音を鳴らそう！
広がったところをたたみ直せば、
また遊べるよ。

**Finished!**
できあがり

Hold ★ tightly
when playing.

遊ぶときは★のあたりを持つよ。

# Ninja Weapon
## しゅりけん

**This is a ninja weapon called "shuriken." It used to be thrown by hand at an enemy. Now, let's become a ninja.**

**1** Ready two pieces of origami.
Fold each paper
and make the cross creases.
Fold both top and bottom sides in half
to meet at the center.
おりがみを2枚用意して、

**1**〜**2**をそれぞれおる。
図のようにおりすじをつけたら上下をおる。

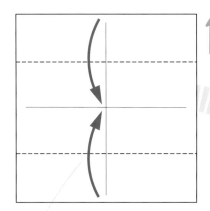

Fold each piece in half.
全体を半分におる。

**2**

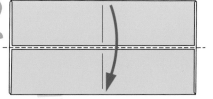

Fold both corners
of each piece.
At this time, be careful
to fold each piece
in different directions.

**3**

角を三角におる。
2枚のおり方がちがうから、図をよく見よう。

**7**

Fold in at the dotted lines, and tuck the tips into the diagonal pockets.

うら返したら、点線のところでおって
先はすきまにさしこむ。

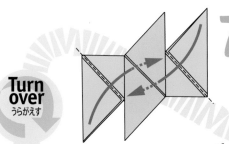

**Turn over**
うらがえす

## Finished!
できあがり

Now I'm a ninja!
にんじゃごっこだ、
シュシュシュッ！

After folding **6**, it will look like this.

**6** をおったところ

**6**

Put one piece on top of the other one and fold in at the dotted lines. Tuck the tips of the triangles into the diagonal pockets.

図のように2つを重ねて
点線のところでおる。
先はすきまにさしこむ。

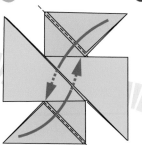

Be careful not to hit someone when you throw it.

人に当たらないように
気をつけてとばそうね。

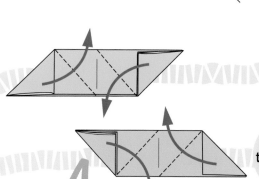

**4**

Fold in at the dotted lines.

おりすじに合わせてそれぞれおる。

**Turn over the lower piece**
下だけうらがえす

Does yours look like this?

下だけうら返したところ。
図と同じになったかな。

**5**

# Sumo Wrestler
## おすもうさん

**Put your sumo wrestlers
on a box and tap the edge.
"Hakkeyoi, nokotta"
means "Fight!"**

**1** Fold in diagonally to make the creases.
Fold in the four corners to meet at the center.
図のようにおりすじをつけたら、
4つの角を中心に向けておる。

**2** Fold both corners
outward to meet
at the center.
中心に合わせて左右を
向こうがわへおる。

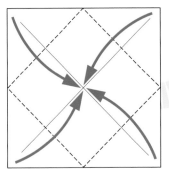

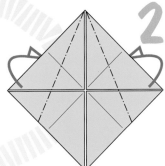

Open up the upper triangles
in the direction of the arrows.
矢じるしのほうへ開く。

**3**

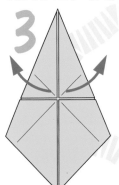

Fold down the top flap at
the dotted line. Fold
the bottom flap outward.
うら返したら、それぞれ
点線のところでおる。

**4**

**Turn
over**
うらがえす

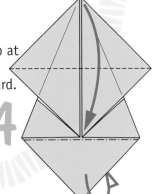

34

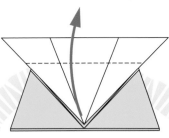

**5** Fold up the upper flap at the dotted line.
点線のところでおり上げる。

After folding **5**, it will look like this.
**5** をおったところ

**Turn over**
うらがえす

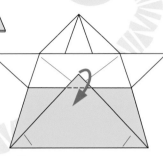

**6** Fold down the tip a little.
とび出たところを
小さくおる。

Fold in half outward.
向こうがわへ
全体を半分におる。

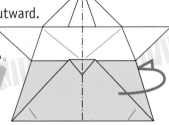

**7**

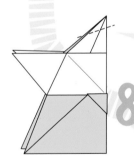

**8** Using the tip, do the outside reverse fold for the head.
外わりおりで「まげ」をおる。

**Finished!**
できあがり

**Play tap-sumo**
とんとんずもうで対戦

Place an empty box upside down to use it as a sumo ring.
Put your figures on it and tap the edge of the box.
The one which goes out of the ring or falls down is the loser.
空き箱の底を上にして土俵をつくり、
おすもうさんをのせて箱のふちをとんとんしよう。
土俵から出たり、倒れちゃったら負けだよ。

35

# Hina Dolls
## おひなさま

If you use Japanese paper, they'll look like real kimonos. The emperor and empress dolls are folded in different ways from halfway.

**1**

After making a crease, fold in both corners to meet at the center.
図のようにおりすじをつけたら、
おりすじに合わせて左右をおる。

**Turn over**
うらがえす

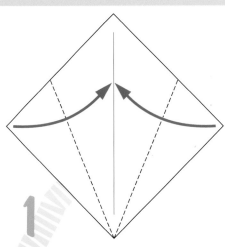

**2**

Fold in both corners at the dotted lines.
うら返したら、
上の左右をおる。

**3**

Fold down in half.
全体を
半分におる。

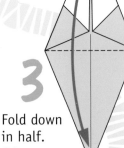

★★

**4**

Fold up the upper flap at the dotted line.
点線のところで
おり上げる。

36

和の伝統おりがみ

**Turn over**
うらがえす

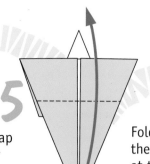

5

Fold up the flap
a little higher
than the other side.

うら返したら、
点線のところでおり上げる。

6

Fold down
the upper flap
at the dotted line.

点線のところでおり下げる。

# Emperor Doll
男びな

# Empress Doll
女びな

Fold up the flap again
so that the top
comes slightly
above
the horizontal line.

点線のところで
おり上げる。

7

7

Tuck in
the triangle part
under the upper flap.

点線のところで内がわにおり入れる。

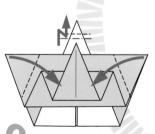

8

Fold in both corners at
the dotted lines.
Fold the pleats to make
the head and crown.

点線のところで両角をおり、
頭はだんおりにする。

8

Fold in both corners
at the dotted lines.
Fold the top outward
and make a flat top
for the head.

点線のところで両角をおり、
頭は山おりにする。

# Finished!
できあがり

# Trick Boat

★★

## だましぶね

You can surprise everyone
with your magic.
Playing with
two persons is fun.

Fold up to step **5** of
the Butterfly (p.20).
ちょうちょ（20ページ）の
**5** までおる。

Fold up the two
upper corners
diagonally at
the dotted lines.
上の2つの角を
おり上げる。

**1**

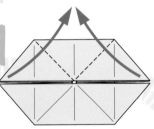

**Turn
over**
うらがえす

After folding **1**,
it will look
like this.

**1** をおったところ

# Can you surprise someone?
うまくだませるかな？

Have someone hold
the sail ★ of the trick
boat and ask him/her
to close his/her eyes.
Pull down the tips
diagonally and...
相手に帆の先★を持って
目をつぶってもらってね。
だます人が2つの角を
ななめにおり下げると……

Fold in diagonally
at the dotted line.
点線のところでななめにおる。

**2**

Hey! I'm holding the bow!

あらふしぎ！
目をあけると、なぜか
「へ先」を持っているよ。

# Finished!
できあがり

# Flapping Bird
## はばたくとり

和の伝統おりがみ

**When you pull the tail,
the bird flaps its wings.**

Fold up to step **7** of
the Crane (p.26).
つる（26ページ）の
**7** までおる。

**1**

Do the inside reverse fold
to make the tail.
At that time, keep it horizontally.
If you fold it up too high,
it won't move smoothly.

中わりおりで尾をおり上げる。
角度を水平くらいにすると、
あとで羽を動かしやすい。

Do the inside reverse
fold for the neck.
中わりおりで
首をおり上げる。

**2**

**Hold ★ in one hand
and pull the tail back
and forth with the other hand.**

★のところを持って、
尾を引っぱったりもどしたりしてね。
パタパタと羽ばたきするよ！

**3**

Do a small inside reverse
fold for the head,
and spread the wings.
小さな中わりおりで
頭をおり、羽は広げる。

## Finished!
できあがり

# Samurai Helmet
## かぶと

**A long time ago,
samurai wore it for a battle.**

※ Double-sided paper. 両面おりがみ使用。

**1** Fold in half to
make a triangle.
角を合わせて半分におる。

**2** Fold in the right and left corners
to meet the bottom corner.
両角を下までおる。

**3** Fold up both flaps
to the top corner.
今度はてっぺんまで
おり上げる。

**4** Fold both flaps
toward
the arrows.
角を外に
向けておる。

**5** Fold up the upper flap
at the dotted line.
手前の1枚を
おり上げる。

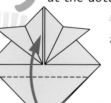

**6** Fold up the flap of **5**
again at the dotted line.
Fold the remaining flap
outward at the dotted line.
手前は点線のところでもう一度おり、
うらの1枚は同じところで向こうへおる。

## Finished!
できあがり

# ★ Goldfish
## きんぎょ

和の伝統おりがみ

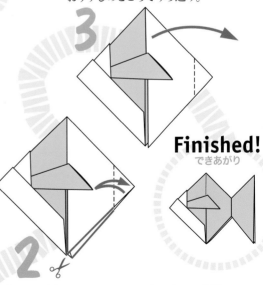

**The big red tail is like that of a real goldfish. You can make this after finishing the Samurai Helmet.**

Fold the Samurai Helmet (p.40) to the end.

かぶと（40ページ）の
できあがりまでおる。

Hold only one piece of the top and pull toward the arrow to fold inside out at the dotted line.

上の1枚を矢じるしのほうへ引き出し、
おりすじのところでうら返す。

**3**

**1**
Put your hand in from ⬆ to open up and flatten from the sides.

下から手を入れて広げ、
横向きにつぶす。

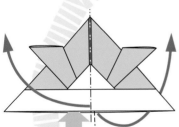

While folding **1**, it will look like this.

**1** を広げているところ

**2**
After making a crease at the dotted line, cut both upper and lower parts as illustrated.

小さな三角をおっておりすじをつけたら、
おりすじまで切りこみを入れる。

# Finished!
できあがり

# Wallet
## さいふ

**Make paper money
and get rich!
You can use it
when pretending to shop.**

Fold the House (p.12)
to the end.
いえ（12ページ）の
できあがりまでおる。

**1**

Fold both sides outward
at the dotted lines.
左右を
向こうがわへ
おる。

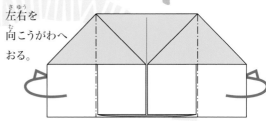

**3**

Fold up the upper flap corner
at the dotted line.
点線のところで
おり上げる。

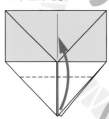

**2**

Fold up the upper flap
corners at the dotted lines.
Repeat on the other side.
手前の1枚の角をななめにおる。
うらも同じに。

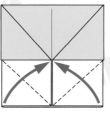

**4**

Fold up again
at the dotted line.
Repeat **3** & **4**
on the other side.
もう一度点線のところでおる。
うらも同じく **3** 〜 **4** をおる。

**Upside
down**
むきをかえる

# Finished!
できあがり

★★

# Petit
# Envelope
## ぽちぶくろ

和の伝統おりがみ

**You can use this envelope when giving someone coins.**

5mm

Ready two different size sheets of paper
and stick them together with glue as illustrated.
大きさのちがう2枚の紙を図のようにはり合わせる。

Make light creases at the center and
at 1/4 of each side.
Fold in at the dotted line and
let the side pass through the center.
ふちの左はしから1/4のところと中心に
しるしをつける。ふちが中心を通るようにおる。

Repeat again.
同じようにおって重ねる。

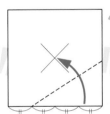

Do the same as **1**
and let the side pass
through the center.
**1**と同じく、ふちが中心を
通るようにおって重ねる。

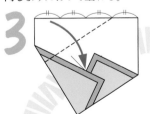

Fold in the last flap at the dotted line.
Fold the short side on the flap of **3**
and tuck in the long side under
the flap of **1**. The flaps will alternate.
最後は一度点線でおってから、はしが
たがいちがいに重なるように◎の紙を上に出す。

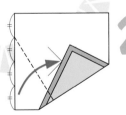

## Finished!
できあがり

★★

# Chopstick Envelope
## and
## Chopstick Rest
### はしぶくろ＆はしおき

**Fold quickly before entertaining guests. Try using beautiful paper.**

## Chopstick Envelope
### はしぶくろ

Ready a 15×15cm sheet of paper.
15×15cm の紙を用意します。

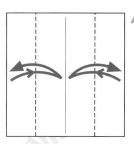

**1** After making a crease at the center, fold in both sides to meet at the center and make the creases.
中心におりすじをつけたら、さらに左右をおっておりすじをつける。

Fold the right side outward for about 5mm.
右はしを 5mm くらいの幅で山おりにする。

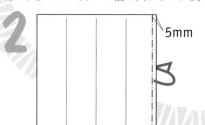

**2**

5mm

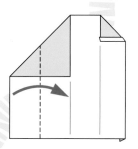

**4** Fold in the left side to the center.
おりすじのところで左をおる。

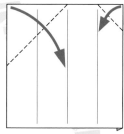

**3** Fold in the upper right corner to make a little triangle.
Fold in the upper left corner to the center and make a big triangle.
左右の角をそれぞれ点線のところでおる。

44

# Chopstick Rest
## はしおき

和の伝統おりがみ

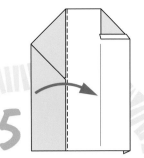

## 5
Fold in to the right again
at the dotted line.
もう一度おりすじの
ところでおる。

Ready a 10×10cm sheet of paper.
Fold the House (p.12) to the end.
10×10cm の紙を用意し、
いえ（12 ページ）のできあがりまでおる。

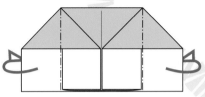

## 1
Fold both sides outward.
左右を向こうがわへおる。

## 6
Fold in the right side on **5**.
右もおりすじのところで
おって重ねる。

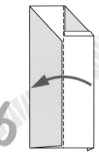

## 2
Fold up the upper flap
twice at the dotted lines.
手前の 1 枚を
点線のところでまくように 2 回おる。

## 7
Fold the bottom
outward.
下を向こうがわへおる。

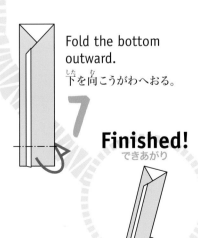

## Finished!
できあがり

## 3
Repeat on the other side.
うらも **2** と同じように
おり上げる。

## Finished!
できあがり

Open the bottom
and flatten the top.
下から指を入れて広げてね。

45

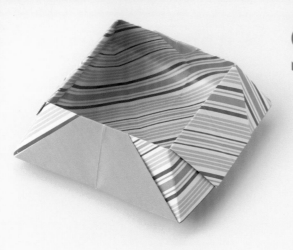

# Sweets Bowl
## かしばち

**How about putting in some candies? You can throw it away when finished.**

Begin with the colored side up and fold up to step **4** of the Crane (p.26).

色のついた面を表にして
つる (26 ページ) の **4** までおる。

Fold the right and left corners of the upper flap to meet at the center. Repeat on the other side.

おりすじに合わせて角をおる。
うらも同じに。

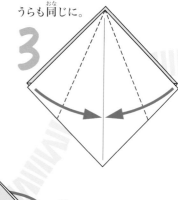

**Upside down**
むきをかえる

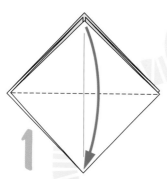

Fold the upper flap down in half. Repeat on the other side.

手前の1枚を半分におる。
うらも同じに。

Fold both sides at the dotted line to change the folding face.

おりずらしておる面をかえる。

和の伝統おりがみ

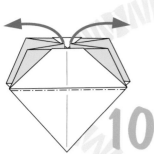

**9**

Fold the tip inside.
Repeat **8** & **9**
on the other side.
とび出た角を内がわに
おりこむ。
うらも同じに **8**〜**9** をおる。

**10**

Fold outward at the dotted line.
Put your finger in
and flatten the bottom.
点線でおって底をつくったら、
広げて形をととのえる。

Fold up
the upper flap
at the dotted line.
点線のところでおり上げる。

**8**

## Finished!
できあがり

Fold both sides
at the dotted line
to change
the folding face.
おりずらしておる面をかえる。

**7**

**6**

Tuck the tip in
the pocket outward.
Repeat on
the other side.
山おりでふくろの中に
おり入れる。うらも同じに。

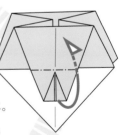

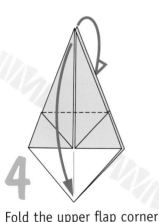

**4**

Fold the upper flap corner
down to the bottom corner.
Repeat on the other side.
角を下までおり下げる。
うらも同じに。

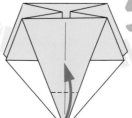

**5**

Fold up the upper flap
at the dotted line.
Repeat on the other side.
点線のところでおり上げる。
うらも同じに。

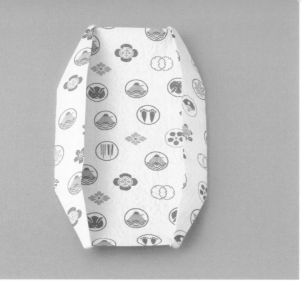

# Tray
トレー

**Use your favorite wrapping paper. Rectangular paper would make a long tray.**

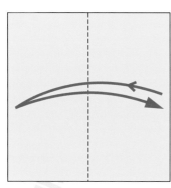

**1**

Begin with the colored side up and make a crease at the center.

色のついた面を表にしておりすじをつける。

**2**

Fold in both sides to meet at the center.

おりすじに合わせて左右をおる。

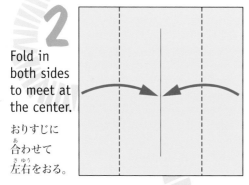

**3**

Fold in both sides again to make the creases.

左右をさらに半分におって、おりすじをつける。

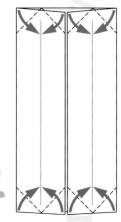

**4**

Fold in the eight corners at the dotted lines.

おりすじに合わせて8つの角をおる。

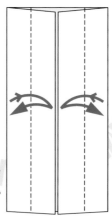

48

## 5
Fold in each corner at the dotted lines again.

それぞれの角をさらにおる。

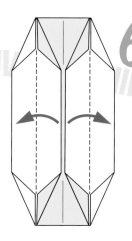

## 6
Open at the center and flatten toward the arrows.

おりすじのところで開く。

**Turn around**
むきをかえる

## 7
After placing it as illustrated, fold both sides outward.

図の向きにかえたら、
両はしを向こうがわへおる。

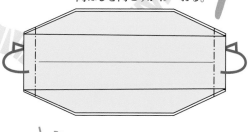

## 8
Lift up the top and bottom sides and flatten the bottom.

わきを起こし、中を広げる。

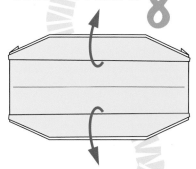

# Finished!
できあがり

It can be used as a container for sweets, stationery, anything you like!

お菓子の器や文房具入れなど、
いろいろに使えるよ！

49

# Horse
## うま

★★

**Long legs are cool!
This origami
came from China.**

Fold up to step **5** of the Crane (p.26).
つる (26 ページ) の **5** までおる。

**1** Cut the upper flap
to the horizontal crease line.
Repeat on the other side.
手前の1枚を
図のようにはさみで切る。
うらも同じに。

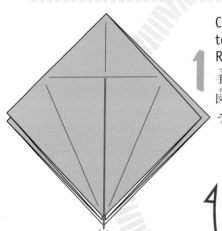

**2** Open up both flaps
at the dotted lines.
Repeat on the other side.
切った三角を、それぞれおり上げる。
うらも同じに。

生きものおりがみ

Fold the upper flaps in half
and repeat on the other side.
These are the legs.
点線のところで、それぞれ半分におる。
うらも同じに。これが足。

**3**

**Upside
down**
むきをかえる

**4**

Turn upside down
and do the inside
reverse fold using
the right flap.
This is the tail.
上下の向きをかえたら、
右を中わりおりにする。

これがしっぽになる。

**5**

Using the left tip,
do the inside
reverse fold.
This is the head.
左は上のほうで
中わりおりにする。
これが頭。

**Finished!**
できあがり

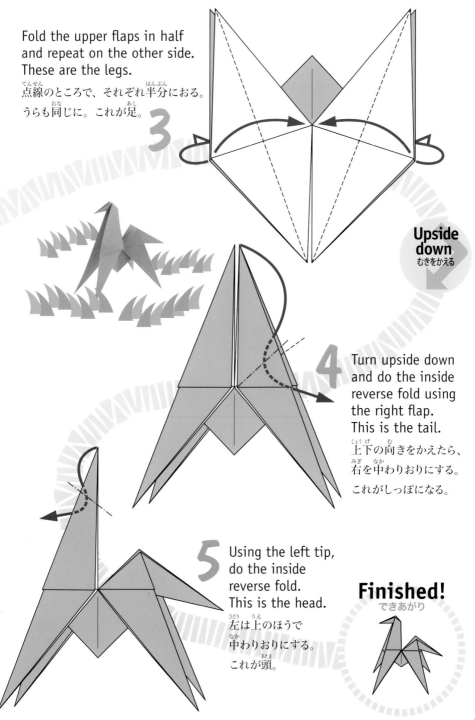

51

# Angelfish

## エンゼルフィッシュ ★★★

Cut a piece of origami
in half and combine
the two triangles.
Let's make a colorful aquarium.

※ Double-sided paper. 両面おりがみ使用。

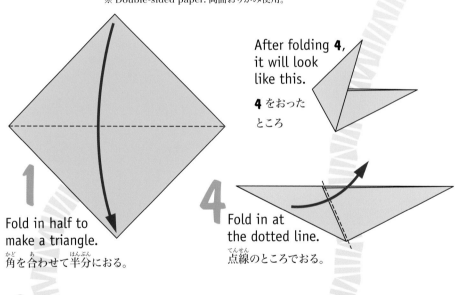

**1** Fold in half to
make a triangle.
角を合わせて半分におる。

**2** Fold up
to make the two sides meet.
辺と辺が合うように、2枚ともおり上げる。

**3** Fold up again
at the dotted line.
もう一度、辺と辺が
合うようにおり上げる。

**4** Fold in at
the dotted line.
点線のところでおる。

After folding **4**,
it will look
like this.
**4** をおった
ところ

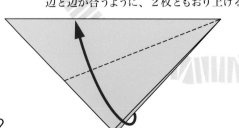

5

Unfold **4** and
cut in half
at the center.

**4** を開き、
中心のおりすじで
半分に切る。

Fold both triangles
along the creases
and go up
to step **4** again.

切りはなした
2枚を
おりすじにそって
もう一度おり直す。

6

**Turn
over**
the lower piece
下だけうらがえす

7

Turn over the lower piece
and combine the two pieces
together.

下だけうら返したら、
2つのパーツを交差させて
組み合わせる。

While combining them,
it will look like this.

**7** を組み合わせて
いるところ

8

Put tail fins together
and fold in and out.

尾びれを重ね合わせて、
たがいちがいになるようにおってとめる。

**Finished!**
できあがり

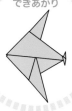

53

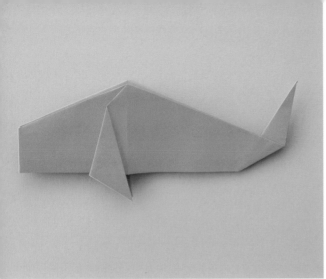

# Carp
## こい

The carp is a familiar fish
in ponds and rivers.
In Japan, you can see
many carp streamers swimming
in the sky in May.

After making a crease,
fold in the top and bottom corners
to meet at the center.
図のようにおりすじをつけたら、
上下をおる。

**1**

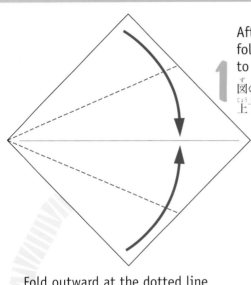

Fold outward at the dotted line
so that the right and left corners meet.
左右の角を合わせるように、
向こうがわへおる。

**2**

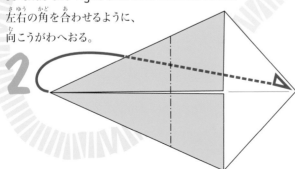

**3**

Put your finger in
from ⬆, and pull up
and flatten toward
the arrow.
⬆から指を入れ、
矢じるしのほうへ
開いてつぶす。

54

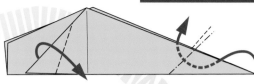

**8** Do the inside reverse fold for the tail, and fold down both side's flaps for the fins.
中わりおりで尾びれをおる。むなびれはおり下げる。

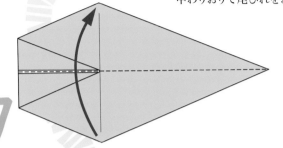

## Finished!
できあがり

**7** Fold up in half from the bottom.
下から半分におり上げる。

**6** Fold in the left corner to the center.
左の角を まん中に合わせておる。

**5** Fold only the upper flap to the left.
上の1枚だけ、左におりたおす。

Repeat on the upper side.
上も同じように開いてつぶす。

**4**

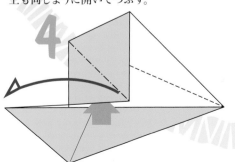

55

# Turtle
## かめ

In Japan, the turtle is associated with good luck, as it is a symbol of long life and happy, harmonious marriage. It often appears in Japanese folklore.

Fold up to step **3** of the Samurai Helmet (p.40).

かぶと（40 ページ）の**3**までおる。

**Fold both corners to meet at the center.**

左右のはしをまん中で
おり合わせる。

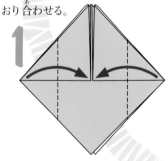

**1**

**Cut the upper flap from the bottom to the middle, and fold the four flaps at the dotted lines.**

手前の１枚にまん中まで切りこみを入れ、
上下の角を外に開く。

**2**

**Finished!**
できあがり

**3**

**Do the pleats fold for the top and bottom to make the head and tail.**

うら返したら、
上下をだんおりにし、
頭としっぽをつくる。

**Turn over**
うらがえす

After folding **2**, it will look like this.

**2**をおったところ

56

★★

# Penguin
## ペンギン

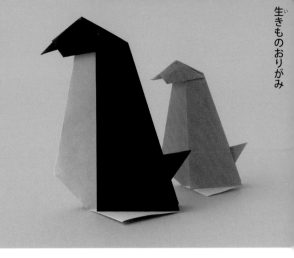

Look, it's going to waddle!
Let's make lots of penguins
and line them up.

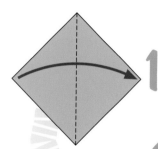

**1** Begin with the colored side up.
Fold in half to make a triangle.
色のついた面を表にして半分におる。

**2** Fold in at the dotted line.
Repeat on the other side.
点線のあたりで谷おりにする。
うらも同じに。

**3** Do the large inside reverse fold
at the dotted line for the tail.
下の角を大きく中わりおりにして、
しっぽをつくる。

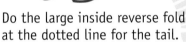

**4** Do the outside
reverse fold.
外わりおりにする。

**5** Fold both bottom
triangles inward and
outward to make legs.
Do the pleats fold
to make the beak.
下の三角は、手前と向こうがわにおる。
頭はだんおりをして、くちばしをおる。

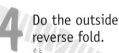

## Finished!
できあがり

# Rooster
## おんどり

**Look at this nice red comb
and these wings!
In Japanese,
a rooster's cry is
"koke-kokko."**

※ Double-sided paper. 両面おりがみ使用。

**1**

Begin with the red side up.
Fold in half to make a triangle.
赤色の面を表にして半分におる。

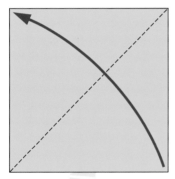

**2**

Fold in half and
make a crease.
半分におって
おりすじをつける。

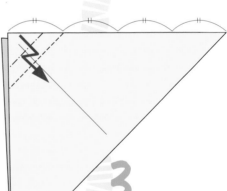

**3**

Fold the upper flap in and
out at the dotted lines.
Fold the tip so that it
sticks out a little.
This is the beak.
手前の1枚をだんおりにする。
角が少しだけ谷おりラインから
とび出すようにする。
ここがくちばしになる。

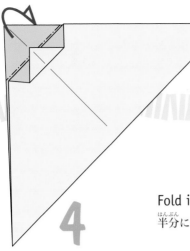

## 4
Fold the bottom flap outward.

うらの1<ruby>枚<rt>まい</rt></ruby>を<ruby>向<rt>む</rt></ruby>こうがわにおる。

## 5
Fold in half.

<ruby>半分<rt>はんぶん</rt></ruby>におる。

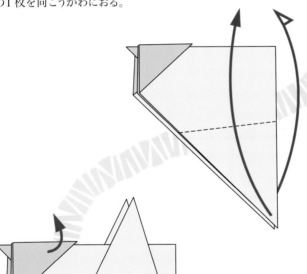

## 6
Fold up both flaps for the wings.

<ruby>羽<rt>はね</rt></ruby>をそれぞれ
おり<ruby>上<rt>あ</rt></ruby>げる。

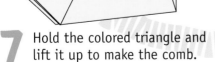

## 7
Hold the colored triangle and lift it up to make the comb.

<ruby>角<rt>かど</rt></ruby>をつまんで<ruby>上<rt>うえ</rt></ruby>に<ruby>引<rt>ひ</rt></ruby>き<ruby>上<rt>あ</rt></ruby>げ、
とさかをつくる。

# Finished!
できあがり

59

# ★★★
# Parakeet
## インコ

If you use double-sided
color origami,
you can make
a wonderful parakeet.

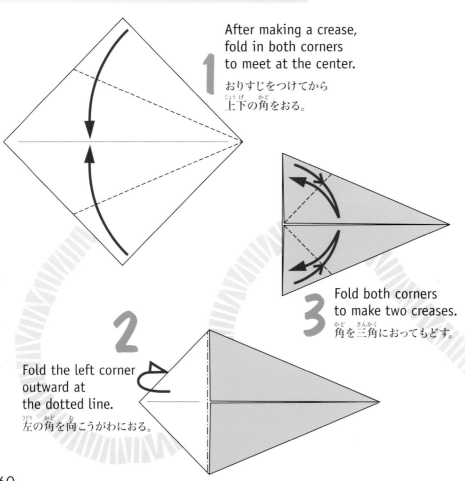

**1** After making a crease,
fold in both corners
to meet at the center.
おりすじをつけてから
上下の角をおる。

**2** Fold the left corner
outward at
the dotted line.
左の角を向こうがわにおる。

**3** Fold both corners
to make two creases.
角を三角におってもどす。

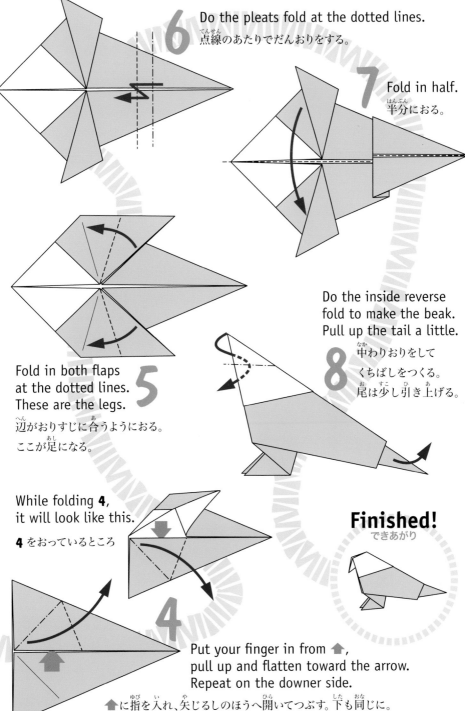

6 Do the pleats fold at the dotted lines.
点線のあたりでだんおりをする。

7 Fold in half.
半分におる。

8 Do the inside reverse fold to make the beak. Pull up the tail a little.
中わりおりをして
くちばしをつくる。
尾は少し引き上げる。

5 Fold in both flaps at the dotted lines. These are the legs.
辺がおりすじに合うようにおる。
ここが足になる。

While folding **4**, it will look like this.
**4** をおっているところ

4 Put your finger in from ⬆, pull up and flatten toward the arrow. Repeat on the downer side.
⬆に指を入れ、矢じるしのほうへ開いてつぶす。下も同じに。

**Finished!**
できあがり

61

# Swallow
## つばめ

**This swallow gliding through the air looks like a real swallow! Make a slit for the long tail.**

Fold up to step **8** of the Crane (p.26).

つる (26ページ) の **8** までおる。

**1**

Fold both sides at the dotted line to change the folding face.

おりずらして
次におる面をかえる。

**2**

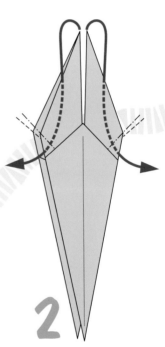

Using both top flaps, do the inside reverse fold. These are the wings.

上の三角をそれぞれ
中わりおりにする。

これがつばさになる。

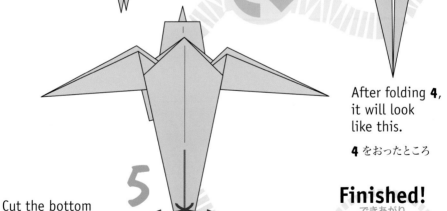

Fold up the upper flap
at the dotted line.

手前の1枚を
点線のあたりで
おり上げる。

*3*

*4*

Do the pleats fold
to make the head
and beak.

だんおりにして、
頭とくちばしをつくる。

**Turn over**
うらがえす

After folding **4**,
it will look
like this.

**4** をおったところ

*5*

Cut the bottom
and cross each flap to
make the tail.

うら返したら
図のように切りこみを入れる。
尾を交差させ、形をととのえる。

**Finished!**
できあがり

# Dragonfly
## とんぼ

★★★

You can make this
when you're halfway
through making the Crane.
Cut the wings in four
and it's finished.

Fold up to step **8**
of the Crane (p.26).
つる（26 ページ）の **8** までおる。

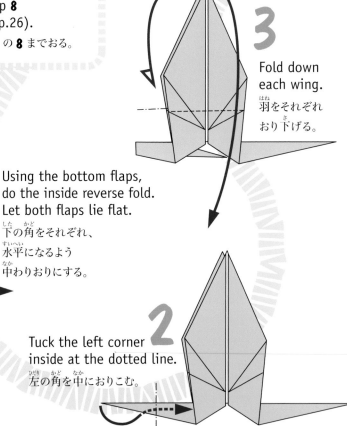

**3**

Fold down
each wing.
羽をそれぞれ
おり下げる。

**1**

Using the bottom flaps,
do the inside reverse fold.
Let both flaps lie flat.
下の角をそれぞれ、
水平になるよう
中わりおりにする。

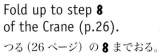

**2**

Tuck the left corner
inside at the dotted line.
左の角を中におりこむ。

生きものおりがみ

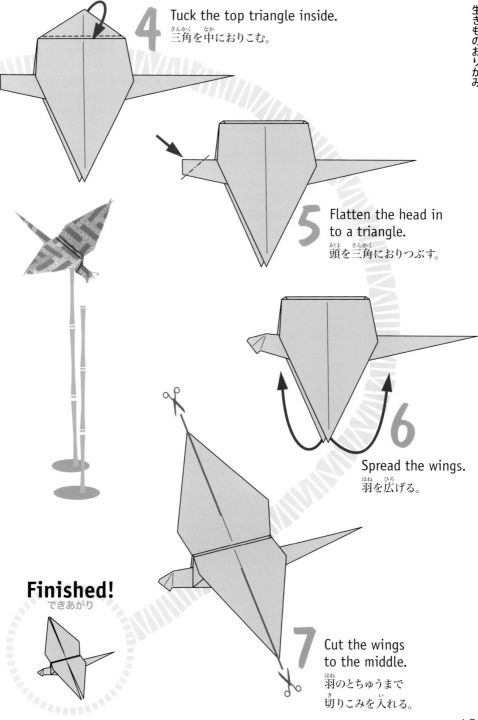

4 Tuck the top triangle inside.
三角を中におりこむ。

5 Flatten the head in to a triangle.
頭を三角におりつぶす。

6 Spread the wings.
羽を広げる。

7 Cut the wings to the middle.
羽のとちゅうまで
切りこみを入れる。

**Finished!**
できあがり

65

# Snail
## かたつむり

**Crawling slowly,
where is it going?
Cut the tip for the antennae.**

**1** After making the diagonal creases,
fold the right and left corners
to meet at the center.

まん中におりすじをつけてから、
左右をおる。

Put your finger in
from ⬆, pull up
and flatten in
the direction of
the arrow.
Repeat on
the other side.

**4**

⬆から指を入れ、矢じるしのほうへ開いてつぶす。
うらも同じに。

**2** Fold in half
so that
the top and
bottom
corners meet.

上下半分におる。

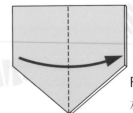

**3**

Fold in half.

左右半分におる。

Fold the right and left corners
to meet at the center.
Repeat on the other side.

おりすじに合わせて
左右をおる。
うらも同じに。

**6**

**7**

Change the folding
face again.
Repeat on
the other side.

おりずらす。うらも同じに。

**5**

Fold both sides
at the dotted line
to change
the folding face.

点線のところでおりずらす。
うらも同じに。

**8**

Use the bottom flaps
to do the inside
reverse fold.

下の角をそれぞれ
中わりおりにする。

# Finished!
できあがり

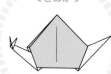

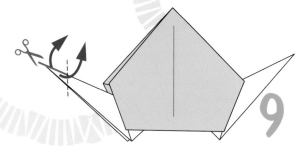

**9**

Cut one tip for the antennae and part the ends.

頭の先に切りこみを入れて、左右に開く。

67

# Grasshopper
## ばった

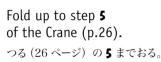

It looks like it's about
to jump from the grass!
When you put one
on top of another,
it looks like a piggyback ride.

Fold up to step **5**
of the Crane (p.26).
つる (26 ページ) の **5** までおる。

Open up the upper flap
and flatten to a diamond shape.
手前の四角の角を上に開き、ひし形につぶす。

**1**

**2**

Fold up both
upper flaps
in the direction
of the arrows.
下から左右におり上げる。

**3**

Fold both
diamond
shapes in half.
左右のひし形を
それぞれ半分におる。

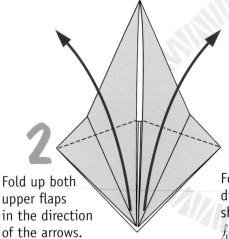

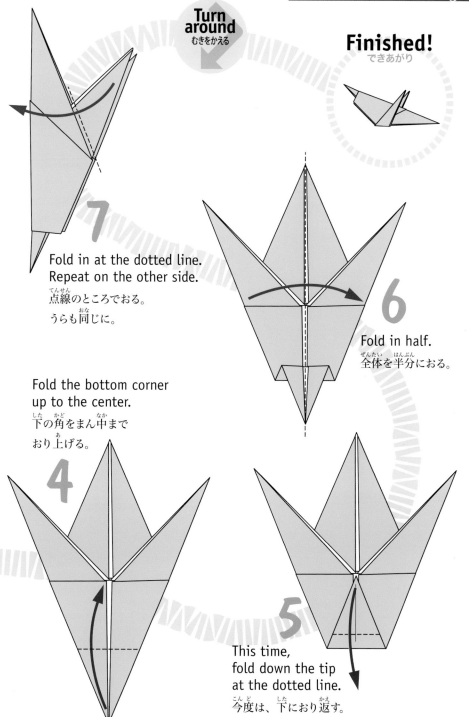

**Turn around**
むきをかえる

**Finished!**
できあがり

## 7

Fold in at the dotted line.
Repeat on the other side.
点線のところでおる。
うらも同じに。

## 6

Fold in half.
全体を半分におる。

Fold the bottom corner
up to the center.
下の角をまん中まで
おり上げる。

## 4

## 5

This time,
fold down the tip
at the dotted line.
今度は、下におり返す。

69

# Strawberry
## いちご

**Use red and green double-sided color paper. Look, it's so pretty!**

※ Double-sided paper. 両面おりがみ使用。

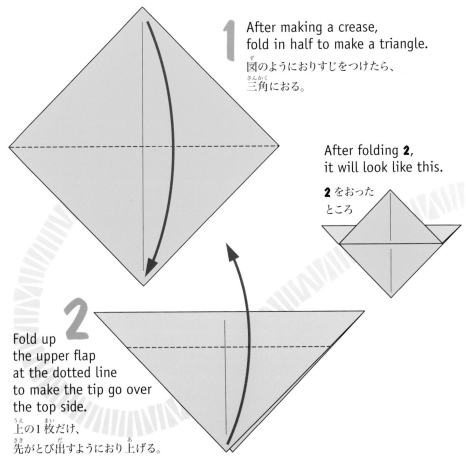

**1** After making a crease, fold in half to make a triangle.
図のようにおりすじをつけたら、三角におる。

After folding **2**, it will look like this.

**2** をおった ところ

**2** Fold up the upper flap at the dotted line to make the tip go over the top side.
上の1枚だけ、先がとび出すようにおり上げる。

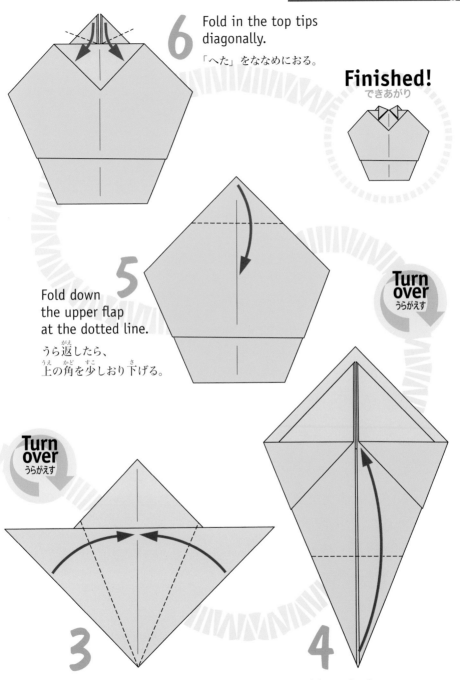

**6** Fold in the top tips diagonally.

「へた」をななめにおる。

**Finished!**
できあがり

**5** Fold down the upper flap at the dotted line.

うら返したら、
上の角を少しおり下げる。

**Turn over**
うらがえす

**Turn over**
うらがえす

**3** Fold in both sides to meet at the center.

うら返したら、おりすじに合わせて左右をおる。

**4** Fold up the bottom corner.

下の角をおり上げる。

71

## ★★

# Morning Glory
## あさがお

**One for a morning glory,
and many for a hydrangea.**

Begin with the colored side up.
Fold up to step **4** of the Crane (p.26).
色のついた面を表にして、
つる (26 ページ) の **4** までおる。

**Upside down**
むきをかえる

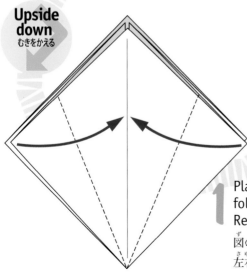

**2**

Cut the top in a curve and
fold up the bottom corner.
上を丸く切り、
下の角はおり上げる。

**1**

Place it as illustrated and
fold in both corners of the upper flap.
Repeat on the other side.
図の向きにおいたら、
左右をおる。うらも同じに。

72

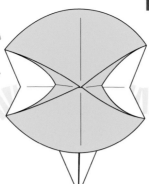

While folding **3**,
it will look like this.
Flatten the right
and left petals.

**3** をおっているところ。
上からおりつぶす。

**Finished!**
できあがり

Put your fingers in from
and open the petals.

から指を入れ、
花びらをおし広げる。

# Two-colored Morning Glory
2色づかいの
あさがお

After folding
**2** with 1/4 size
paper (don't cut
the top),
insert it inside the bigger flower
and open the petals.

1/4 ほどの大きさの紙で
**1**、**2** と同じように
おったら（こちらは
先を丸く切らない）、
花びらの中にさしこんで、
あとは **3**、**4** と同じにおる。

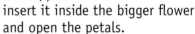

## Fold tiny paper to make a hydrangea.
小さい紙でおって、あじさいに

Fold many flowers with tiny pieces
(don't cut the top) and
paste them together with glue.

**2** で先を切らないまま、小さな紙で
たくさん小花をつくってはり合わせよう。

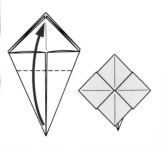

★★

# Jumping Frog
## ぴょんぴょんがえる

**Flip the fold and
the frog will jump!
Which can jump the furthest?**

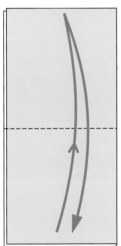

# 1
Fold the opposing
two sides in half
and make a crease.
横半分におってから、
図のように
おりすじをつける。

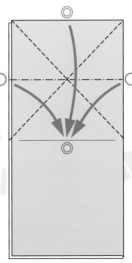

# 2
Make three creases
as illustrated.
Fold in so that ○ meets ○
and ◎ meets ◎ ,
and make a triangle top.
点線のとおりに
おりすじをつけたら、
○と○、◎と◎が合うように、
おりたたむ。

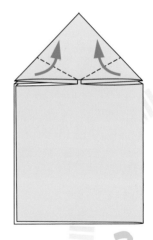

# 3
Fold up
the upper triangles
to make
the front legs.
手前の三角をおり上げて、
前足をつくる。

**Put your finger on the back
and release it to make the frog jump.**

指をバネの上にのせて、

はじいてみてね。

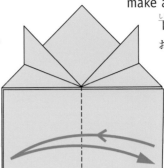

**Fold in
the bottom part and
make a crease.**

下半分だけおって、

おりすじをつける。

5

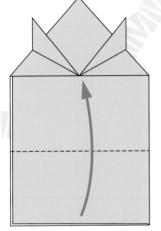

**Fold in both sides
to meet at
the center.**

おりすじに合わせて
左右をおる。

6

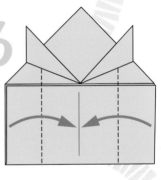

**Fold up the bottom
at the dotted line.**

点線のところでおり上げる。

4

# Finished!

できあがり

**Do the pleats fold
at the dotted lines.
This works
as the spring.**

図のように

だんおりをする。

ここがバネになる。

7

**Turn
over**

うらがえす

**After folding 7,
it will look like this.**

**7** をおったところ

75

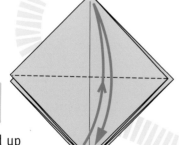

# Tree-climbing Monkey

★★

## さるのきのぼり

**Look! A monkey climbs up the tree and shows its face at the top. What fun!**

*The monkey appears at the top!*
てっぺんから顔を出した！

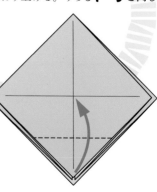

ぴょこん！

※ Double-sided paper. 両面おりがみ使用。

Begin with the green side up.
Fold up to step **4**
of the Crane (p.26).
緑色の面を表にして、
つる（26 ページ）の **4** までおる。

**3**

Fold up twice
at the dotted lines.
Repeat **1** to **3**
on the other side.
巻くように2回、おり上げる。うらも **1** 〜 **3** と同じに。

**1**

Fold up
the upper flap
to make a crease.
手前の1枚を半分におって
もどし、
おりすじをつける。

**2**

Fold in
the bottom corner
to the center.
中心に向けて角をおる。

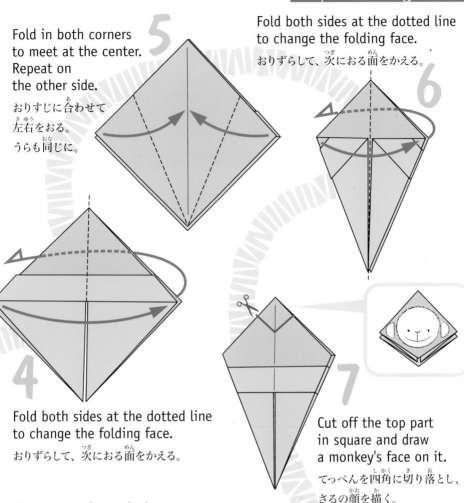

**5** Fold in both corners to meet at the center. Repeat on the other side.

おりすじに合わせて左右をおる。うらも同じに。

**6** Fold both sides at the dotted line to change the folding face.

おりずらして、次におる面をかえる。

**4** Fold both sides at the dotted line to change the folding face.

おりずらして、次におる面をかえる。

**7** Cut off the top part in square and draw a monkey's face on it.

てっぺんを四角に切り落とし、さるの顔を描く。

You can make variations, such as lava erupting from a volcano, by changing the colors of paper. Give it a try!

色をかえて、火山とよう岩などいろいろためそう。

**Bang!!**

Put the monkey in the slit of the tree and rub both sides.

さるを木の間にはさんだら木と木をこすり合わせるよ。

**Finished!**
できあがり

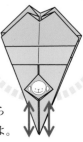

77

★★

# Medal
## くんしょう

**Decorate it with ribbons
and seals and
give it as a present
for a job well done.**

Fold up to step **5** of the Butterfly (p.20).
ちょうちょ（20ページ）の**5**までおる。

**1**

Open up and flatten
the upper right triangle
toward the arrow.
Do the same for the other
three triangles.
右上の三角を、矢じるしの
ほうへ開いてつぶす。
ほかの3カ所も同じに。

**2** Make eight thin triangles
along the diagonal creases.
ななめのおりすじに合わせて、
細い三角を8つおる。

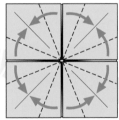

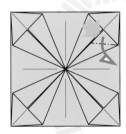

**3** Open and flatten
the triangle pocket.
Do the same for
the other seven triangles.
三角のふくろを開いてつぶす。
ほかの7つも同じに。

**4** Fold the four corners outward.
4つの角を向こうがわにおる。

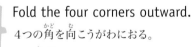

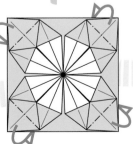

# Finished!
できあがり

78

遊べるおりがみ

# Necktie
## ネクタイ

★★

What kind of necktie would you make?
It's a perfect present for Father's Day.
Large paper would make one
just like a real necktie.

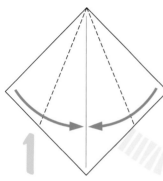

**1** After making a crease, fold both corners to meet at the center.
図のようにおりすじを
つけたら、左右をおる。

**2** Do the pleats fold at the dotted lines.
点線のあたりでだんおりにする。

**3** Fold in at the dotted line over the center line.
点線のところで
内がわに
中心線を
こえておる。

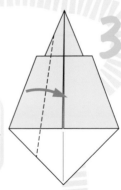

**5** Fold in the top corner.
先をおる。

**4** Put your finger in from ⬆, pull up and flatten toward the arrow. Repeat **3** & **4** on the right side.
⬆に指を入れ、矢じるしのほうへ
開いてつぶす。
右がわも同じように、**3**〜**4**をおる。

**Turn over**
うらがえす

**Finished!**
できあがり

79

# Shirt
シャツ

Use a large rectangular paper.
Everyone will be surprised
when you send them
a letter folded like this!

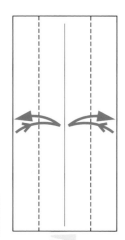

**1**

After making a center crease
on a rectangular paper,
fold the opposing two sides
in half and unfold.

長方形の紙のまん中におりすじを
つけたら、左右をおって、
さらにおりすじをつける。

Fold in both sides
at the dotted lines
to meet at the center.

おりすじに合わせて
左右をおる。

**3**

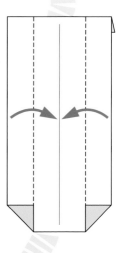

**2**

Fold in the bottom corners
at the dotted lines.
Fold the top side outward
for the collar.

下の角は内がわへおり、
上は細めに山おりにする。

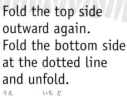

**4**

Fold the top side
outward again.
Fold the bottom side
at the dotted line
and unfold.

上はもう一度
向こうがわにおり、
下はおりすじだけ

つける。

**5**

Fold up the bottom ○
to the upper ○.
These are the sleeves.

矢じるしのほうへ
開いてつぶし、○と○が
重なるようにおる。

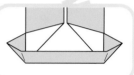

While folding **5**,
it will look like this.

**5**をおっているところ

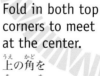

**7**

Fold up
the bottom side
and tuck it under
the collar.

下からおり上げて、
えり下にさしこむ。

Fold in both top
corners to meet
at the center.

上の角を
合わせ目までおって、
えりをつくる。

**6**

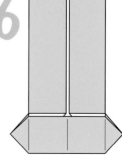

# Finished!

できあがり

81

# Watch
## うでどけい

**Amazing!**
**You can even make a cube**
**from a piece of paper.**
**Draw the clockface and**
**then make the final shape.**

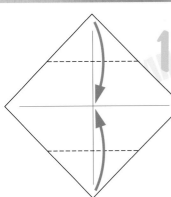

**1** After making the diagonal creases,
fold in both top and bottom corners
to meet at the center.
まん中におりすじをつけてから、上下をおる。

Fold in both sides
again to meet at
the center.
もう一度、
上下をおる。

**2**

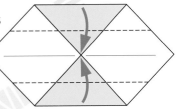

**3**

Fold in half outward
at the dotted line.
向こうがわに半分におる。

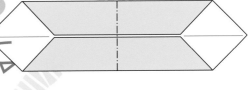

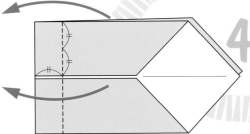

**4** Fold back to the left side
at the dotted line.
Repeat on the other side.
点線のところで左におり返す。
うらも同じに。

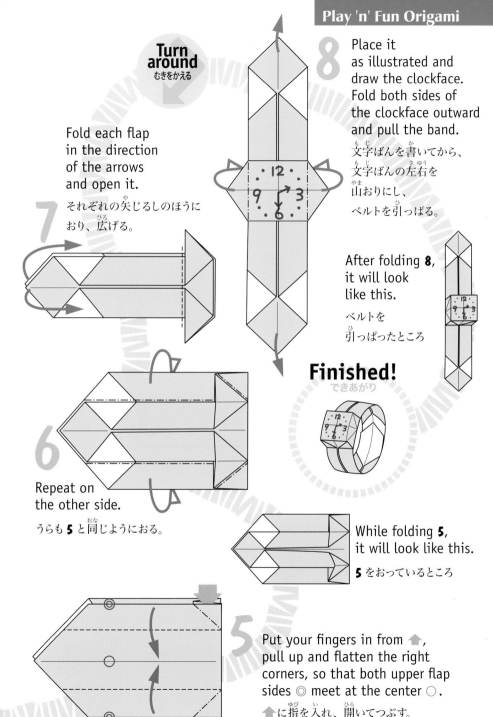

**Turn around**
むきをかえる

Fold each flap
in the direction
of the arrows
and open it.

それぞれの矢じるしのほうに
おり、広げる。

**7**

**8**
Place it
as illustrated and
draw the clockface.
Fold both sides of
the clockface outward
and pull the band.

文字ばんを書いてから、
文字ばんの左右を
山おりにし、
ベルトを引っぱる。

・12・
9    3
・6・

After folding **8**,
it will look
like this.

ベルトを
引っぱったところ

**Finished!**
できあがり

**6**

Repeat on
the other side.

うらも **5** と同じようにおる。

While folding **5**,
it will look like this.

**5** をおっているところ

**5**

Put your fingers in from ⬆,
pull up and flatten the right
corners, so that both upper flap
sides ◎ meet at the center ○.

⬆に指を入れ、開いてつぶす。
◎の辺はおりすじ○にそうように。

83

# Handbag
## ハンドバッグ

It's cubic and has
a wide bottom.
When you use
a large piece of paper,
you can really use it as a bag.

Begin with the colored side up.
Fold up to step **4** of the Crane (p.26).
色のついた面を表にして、
つる（26 ページ）の **4** までおる。

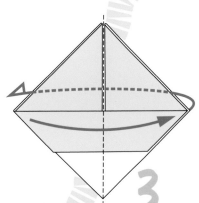

**Upside
down**
むきをかえる

**3**

Fold both sides at
the dotted line to change
the folding face.
おりずらして、次におる面をかえる。

**1**

Place it as illustrated
and fold down
the upper flap
to make a crease.
図の向きにしたら、
手前の1枚に
おりすじをつける。

**2**

Fold in the upper corner
to the center and
fold in again.
Repeat **1** & **2**
on the other side.
上の角をまん中に向けており、
さらにおりすじのところでおる。
うらも **1**〜**2** と同じに。

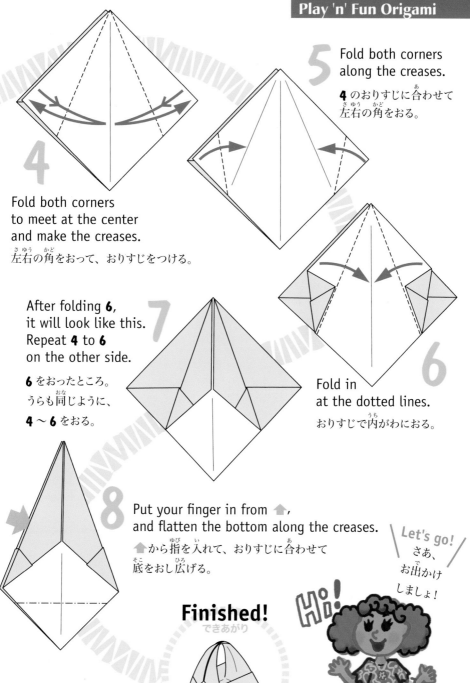

**4**

Fold both corners
to meet at the center
and make the creases.
左右の角をおって、おりすじをつける。

**5**

Fold both corners
along the creases.
**4** のおりすじに合わせて
左右の角をおる。

**6**

Fold in
at the dotted lines.
おりすじで内がわにおる。

**7**

After folding **6**,
it will look like this.
Repeat **4** to **6**
on the other side.

**6** をおったところ。
うらも同じように、
**4** 〜 **6** をおる。

**8**

Put your finger in from ⬆,
and flatten the bottom along the creases.
⬆から指を入れて、おりすじに合わせて
底をおし広げる。

Let's go!
さあ、
お出かけ
しましょ！

**Finished!**
できあがり

Use glue for the handle!
バッグの持ち手をのりでとめよう！

85

# Ribbon

リボン

How about using it
as a hair ornament?
Let's use all kinds of
colorful paper.

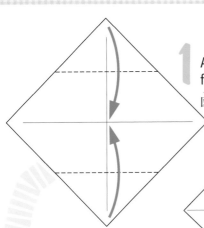

**1** After making the diagonal creases,
fold in both corners to meet at the center.
図のようにおりすじをつけたら、上下の角をおる。

**3** Fold in half.
半分におる。

**2** Fold in again along
the crease.

おりすじに合わせて
上下をおる。

Fasten it with
a hairpin and there!
You have
a lovely hair ornament.

ピンでとめたら、すてきなかみかざりに！

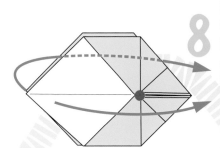

**8** Pressing both sides of ●
so that the folds will not open,
pull both flaps.

おり目<sub>め</sub>が開<sub>ひら</sub>かないように●のところを押<sub>お</sub>さえながら、
両<sub>りょう</sub>がわに引<sub>ひ</sub>っぱる。

**7** Fold both corners
to meet at the center.
Repeat on
the other side.

角<sub>かど</sub>をおる。うらも同<sub>おな</sub>じに。

## Finished!
できあがり

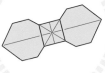

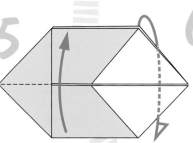

**6** Fold back each flap
at the dotted line.

点線<sub>てんせん</sub>のところで
おり返<sub>かえ</sub>す。

**5** Fold both sides
at the dotted line
to change
the folding face.

おりずらして、
次<sub>つぎ</sub>におる面<sub>めん</sub>をかえる。

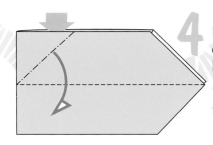

**4** Put your finger in from ⬆,
open and flatten toward the arrow.
Repeat on the other side.

⬆から指<sub>ゆび</sub>を入<sub>い</sub>れて、
矢<sub>や</sub>じるしのほうへ開<sub>ひら</sub>いてつぶす。
うらも同<sub>おな</sub>じに。

# Cup
## コップ

**Folding with
juice colored paper is fun.
Use it when playing house.**

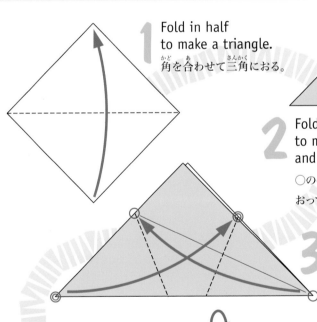

**1** Fold in half
to make a triangle.
角を合わせて三角におる。

**2** Fold the upper flap side down
to meet the bottom side
and make a crease.
○の2つの辺が合うように
おってもどし、おりすじをつける。

**3** Fold in both corners
so that ○ meets ○
and ◎ meets ◎.
○と○、◎と◎が合うように
左右の角をおる。

**4** Fold the upper flap in
and the other flap
outward.
手前の1枚を谷おりに、
残りの1枚は山おりにする。

## Finished!
できあがり

88

# Yacht
ヨット

遊べるおりがみ

The big triangular sail makes
it look like it's in full sail.
What kind of mark are
you going to draw on the sail?

After making a crease,
fold up the bottom side.
図のようにつけた
おりすじに合わせて、
下をおり上げる。

**1**

Fold the left corner
outward to meet
the right corner.
左の角が右の角に
合うように、
向こうがわにおる。

**2**

Put your finger in from ⬆,
pull up and flatten
toward the arrow.
⬆に指を入れ、
矢じるしのほうへ
開いてつぶす。

**3**

# Finished!
できあがり

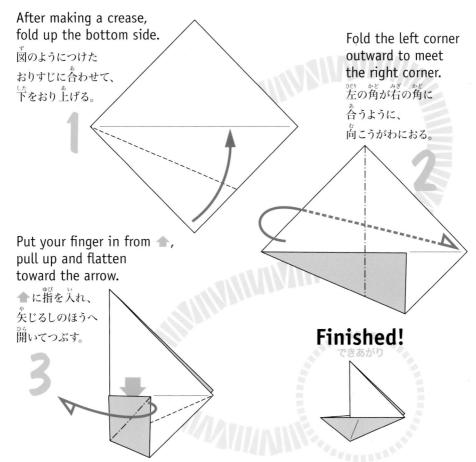

## ★★
# Wind Boat
## ウインドボート

**The boat will glide**
**when you blow into the sail.**

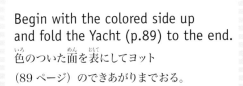

Begin with the colored side up
and fold the Yacht (p.89) to the end.
色のついた面を表にしてヨット
(89 ページ) のできあがりまでおる。

Open the lower flap
to the left side.
向こうがわの1枚を
左へ開く。

**1**

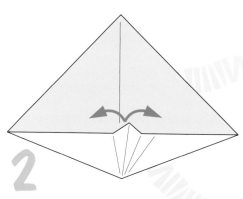

**2**

Fold the horn right and left
to make it stand upright.
まん中のツノを左右におり、
立つようにする。

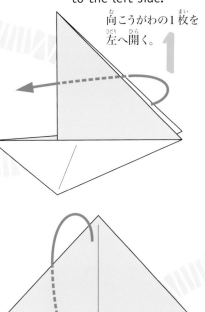

**3**

Fold outward
at the dotted line.
点線のところで山おりにする。

遊べるおりがみ

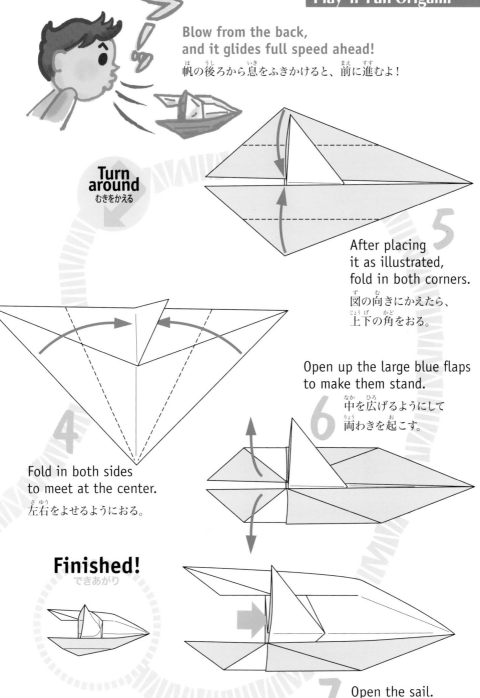

**Blow from the back,
and it glides full speed ahead!**

帆の後ろから息をふきかけると、前に進むよ！

**Turn
around**
むきをかえる

**5**
After placing
it as illustrated,
fold in both corners.

図の向きにかえたら、
上下の角をおる。

**6**
Open up the large blue flaps
to make them stand.

中を広げるようにして
両わきを起こす。

**4**
Fold in both sides
to meet at the center.

左右をよせるようにおる。

**Finished!**
できあがり

**7**
Open the sail.

帆を広げる。

91

# Rocket
ロケット

★★

**Blow into it with a straw.
Three, two, one, lift off!
Flying far out into space!**

Fold up to step **4** of the Balloon (p.10).
ふうせん（10 ページ）の **4** までおる。

Fold in both upper sides so that
each ○ meets at ◎ along the crease.
○の辺が◎のおりすじと合うように、
左右を三角におる。

**1**

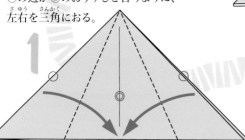

**2**

After folding **1**,
it will look like this.
Repeat on the other side.

**1**をおったところ。うらも同じに。

Insert a flex straw
from under the bottom,
and blow fully into it
to let the rocket lift off!
曲がるストローを下からさしこんで
思いっきりふいて飛ばそう！

**3** Fold in the upper corners to meet at the center.

まん中<sub>なか</sub>で合<sub>あ</sub>うように角<sub>かど</sub>をおる。

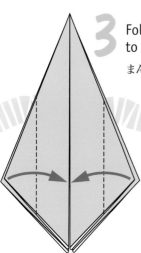

**4** After folding **3**, it will look like this. Repeat on the other side.

**3** をおったところ。うらも同<sub>おな</sub>じに。

**7** Put your finger in from under the bottom, opening and shaping it.

下<sub>した</sub>から指<sub>ゆび</sub>を入<sub>い</sub>れて中<sub>なか</sub>を広<sub>ひろ</sub>げる。

**5** Fold the bottom triangles outward at the dotted lines.

下<sub>した</sub>の三角<sub>さんかく</sub>を開<sub>ひら</sub>くように外<sub>そと</sub>がわにおる。

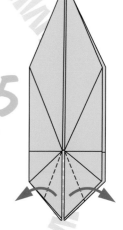

# Finished!
できあがり

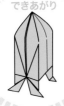

**6** After folding **5**, it will look like this. Repeat on the other side.

**5** をおったところ。うらも同<sub>おな</sub>じに。

# Index

# さくいん（50音順）

## How to make a square with a large piece of paper
### 大きな紙でおるときは

You can make a square easily from newspaper or wrapping paper.
Let's try the Samurai Helmet or Handbag with a large piece of paper.

新聞紙や包そう紙などから簡単に正方形がつくれます。
大きな紙で「かぶと」や「ハンドバッグ」などをおってみましょう。

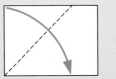

Fold in one top corner to the bottom side and make a triangle.

辺と辺を合わせて三角におる。

Cut off the rectangular part and unfold the triangle.

切って三角を広げると正方形に。

**Cut here.** ここを切るよ。

ブックデザイン／落合光恵
表紙ロゴデザイン（Cool Japan）／鈴木住枝（コンセント）
イラスト／手塚由紀
作品製作／鈴木キャシー裕子　唐木順子
折図トレース／西紋三千代　竜崎あゆみ
撮影／鈴木江実子　松木 潤（主婦の友社写真課）
構成・編集／鈴木キャシー裕子
校正／田杭雅子　伊藤優子（共同制作社）
編集協力／高橋容子
編集担当／松本可絵（主婦の友社）

# 英語訳つき
# おりがみ Best 50

訳　者　青木真理
編　者　主婦の友社
発行者　荻野善之
発行所　株式会社 主婦の友社
　　　　〒101-8911 東京都千代田区神田駿河台2-9
　　　　電話　03-5280-7537（編集）
　　　　　　　03-5280-7551（販売）
印刷所　大日本印刷株式会社

＊本書は『英語訳つき人気のおりがみ Best 50』（2011年刊）を再編集したものです。

●乱丁本、落丁本はおとりかえします。お買い求めの書店か、主婦の友社資材刊行課（電話03-5280-7590）にご連絡ください。
●内容に関するお問い合わせは、主婦の友社（電話03-5280-7537）まで。
●主婦の友社が発行する書籍・ムックのご注文は、お近くの書店か主婦の友社コールセンター（電話0120-916-892）まで。
＊お問い合わせ受付時間　月～金（祝日を除く）　9:30～17:30
主婦の友社ホームページ　http://www.shufunotomo.co.jp/

© SHUFUNOTOMO CO.,LTD. 2016 Printed in Japan
ISBN978-4-07-418461-3
Ⓡ本書を無断で複写複製（電子化を含む）することは、著作権法上の例外を除き、禁じられています。本書をコピーされる場合は、事前に公益社団法人日本複製権センター（JRRC）の許諾を受けてください。
また本書を代行業者等の第三者に依頼してスキャンやデジタル化することは、たとえ個人や家庭内での利用であっても一切認められておりません。
JRRC〈 http://www.jrrc.or.jp　e メール：jrrc_info@jrrc.or.jp　電話：03-3401-2382 〉

た-121001